Biblical Illiteracy in American Teaching Institutions

A Systemic Problem in Families, Churches, and Schools

Dr. Timothy Gordon

First paperback edition April 2021

ISBN: 9798738191084

http://ii4rsc.org

TABLE OF CONTENTS

TABLE OF CONTENTS 1
CHAPTER 1 INTRODUCTION 5
    Definitions.. 5
        Bible Literacy.. 5
        Biblical Illiteracy 6
    The Problem of Biblical Illiteracy... 7
        Biblical Illiteracy in Christian Families.................................... 7
        Biblical Illiteracy in Christian Churches and Schools.......... 9
        Biblical Illiteracy in Secular Schools.. 12
CHAPTER 2 SIGNIFICANT BIBLE PASSAGES 14
    Hosea 4:6 14
    Isaiah 1:2-3; 5:12-13 15
    Acts 17:30-31 17
    Hebrews 5:11-14 18
CHAPTER 3 A BRIEF SURVEY OF BIBLE ORIGINS, SIGNIFICANCE & LITERACY 19
    Bible the Most Published and Printed Yet Misunderstood and Misinterpreted Book.. 19
    Geneva Bible the Bible of Puritans, Pilgrims, and Protestant Reformation 20
    The Bible Available to Virtually 99% of World's People 21
    Bible Literacy Polls and Technology 21
CHAPTER 4 SOME FACTORS THAT CAUSE BIBLICAL ILLITERACY 23
    Only Half of Pastors and 9% of Adults Have a Biblical Worldview 23
    Biblical Illiteracy, Theological Heterodoxy, and Moral Frailty................. 25
    Pastors and Teachers Must Contextualize in a Post-Christian Postmodern Era 25
    Information Overload and Biblical Illiteracy 26
    Being Relevant, Situation Ethics, and Biblical Illiteracy 26
    The Diminishing Role of Biblical Preaching and Teaching in Churches 27
    The Failure of the Church to Transmit Religious Culture to Next Generation... 27
    The Influence of Unbiblical Philosophies and Worldviews on Biblical Illiteracy.. 28
CHAPTER 5 SOME CONSEQUENCES OF BIBLICAL ILLITERACY 29
    Perfect Candidates for Cults, Human Philosophies, and World Religions.. 29
    The Biblically Illiterate are Silent in the Face of Evil or Error 30
    Women Traditionally the Spiritual Leaders, Mentors, and Role Models 30
    Biblically Illiterate Men Lack Spiritual Leadership 31
    Biblical Illiteracy Poisons Individuals, Churches, and Communities 31

Bible Ignorance Perpetuated By Distorted Cartoons and Movies............32
CHAPTER 6 SUMMARY AND CONCLUSIONS..**33**
Summary..33
Conclusions 34
Barna Research Shows Recent Hopeful Trends Without Transition in Beliefs..34
Barna Encouraged by Decade of Increased Religious Behaviors 34
Bible Literates Will Never Dominate the Church 35
The Problem of Biblical Illiteracy Will Never Disappear.................35
APPENDIX A SOME RECOMMENDED SOLUTIONS FOR BIBLICAL ILLITERACY **36**
Bible Literary Requires Reinforcement and Repetition 36
Congregational Leadership Must Make Biblical Illiteracy Top Priority..36
Bible Reading, Study, Parents, Preachers the Antidote to Biblical Illiteracy...37
Voluntary, Informal Bible Study Better Predictor of Biblical Knowledge...38
Study Shows Correlation Between Church Position and Education Level 38
Leaders Must Diagnose Problems, Reconstruct Educational Ministry, Identify Teachers...39
Establish Bible Electives in High School — College Students Next Great Awakening...40
Churches Must Recover Centrality and Urgency of Biblical Teaching and Preaching 41
Churches Must Use Revelation/Response Education, Presence/ Presentation Evangelism..41
Churches Must Affirm Authority of God's Word, Read Bible With Expectancy, Model...42
Marlowe's Ten Steps to Biblical Literacy...43
Leaders Must Acknowledge, Evaluate, Instruct, Alert, Encourage 45
APPENDIX B ORGANIZATIONS THAT PROMOTE BIBLE LITERACY PROGRAMS **47**
Bible Literacy Project...47
National Council on Bible Curriculum in Public Schools 47
The Bible Literacy Center..48
Back to the Bible..48
APPENDIX C JAMES ENGLE SPIRITUAL DECISION-MAKING MODEL **50**
WORKS CITED **51**
SELECTED BIBLIOGRAPHY **57**

CHAPTER 1

INTRODUCTION

This book is an investigation of the systemic problem of biblical illiteracy in American families, churches, and schools. The research is primarily religious in nature and most data are from Christian sources although research from secular schools and polls is used. Bible literacy and biblical illiteracy definitions are defined from existing research or derived from observations by pastoral and educational experts. An exposition of several appropriate Bible passages from both the Old and New Testaments are presented to reveal the nature of biblical illiteracy. A brief survey of the origin, significance, and literacy of the Bible is evaluated for the background information. Some factors that cause biblical illiteracy from different sources will be evaluated to determine the possible causes of biblical illiteracy. Some consequences of biblical illiteracy from different experts in pastoral and educational fields will be examined and discussed. Some recommended solutions for biblical illiteracy are included under Appendix A. Appendix B is provided for informational purposes to facilitate readers who might need resources about organizations that sponsor and promote Bible literacy. James Engle's revolutionary spiritual decision-making model is included as Appendix C.

Definitions

Bible Literacy

There are no standard definitions for Bible literacy. The Merriam-Webster's Dictionary defines *literate* as "having knowledge or competence."[1] Therefore, one can simply define Bible literacy as "having knowledge or competence with the Bible." A pastor might define Bible literacy as the minimum knowledge that one needs for salvation and how to live. Forty teachers interviewed by the Bible Literacy Project have defined Bible literacy as composed of the following five components: (a) knowing the book the Bible, (b) being familiar with common Bible stories, (c) being familiar with popular Bible characters, (d) being able to recognize common biblical phrases, and (e) being able to connect that knowledge to references in literature.[2]

Biblical Illiteracy

Merriam-Webster's Dictionary defines *illiterate* as "showing or marked by a lack of acquaintance with the fundamentals of a particular field of knowledge."[3] The noun *functional illiterate* is defined as "a person who has had some schooling but does not meet a minimum standard of literacy."[4] A working definition of biblical illiteracy might be, "lacking the minimum Bible knowledge fundamentals that one needs to be saved and how to live in this world." Charles Nichols defines biblical illiteracy as both a functional and cognitive problem.[5] In his essay he concludes that Isaiah 5:13, Hosea 4:6, and James 1:21-22 all describe an illiteracy that is functional because Israel knew about God but rejected him and illiteracy that is cognitive because Christians do not know the content of Scripture and consequently, cannot apply it.[6]

---

[1] Merriam-Webster's 11th Collegiate Dictionary (2003), s.v. "literate."
[2] The Gallup Organization, *Teenagers' Knowledge of the Bible, The Bible Literacy Report: What Do American Teens Need to Know and What Do They Know?* (New York City: Bible Literacy Project, 2005), 19.
[3] Merriam-Webster's 11th Collegiate Dictionary (2003), s.v. "illiterate."
[4] Ibid., s.v. "functional illiterate."
[5] Charles H. Nichols, "Communicating to a Biblically Illiterate World," *Didaskalia* 4, no. 2 (April 1993): 2-4 [journal on-line]; available from http://newfirstsearch.oclc.org; Internet; accessed 2 July 2006.
[6] Ibid.

The Problem of Biblical Illiteracy

Biblical Illiteracy in Christian Families

The responsibility of teaching children in any context begins in the family—it is the foundational teaching institution for children. The issue of Bible literacy has its foundation in the family. Therefore, the problem of biblical illiteracy begins with the family.

Lillian Daniel, who pastors a New England Congregational church, says you can never assume there is biblical literacy within the families of the congregation. She describes the dynamics of the problem in this way:

> Increasingly, people wander into our church with a similar story. They were raised by parents who believed children ought to "choose their religion for themselves." They had parents of different faiths or no faith who preached a generic morality across the dinner table in the hope that something would sink in. Then, after these children were old enough to have busy social schedules, they were offered the option of attending religious institutions their parents had thus far ignored. . . . Few praise their parents for raising them without any religious training. They have been left without a framework in which to consider life's mysteries, and when they do enter a church, they feel illiterate.[7]

Albert Mohler, President of The Southern Baptist Theological Seminary, argues that biblical illiteracy is the problem of the church and the recovery begins at home. Note his comments on this:

---

[7] Lillian Daniel, "I Love to Tell the Story to Those Who Know It Least," *Christianity Today*, 43, no. 9 (August 9, 2006): 49 [journal on-line]; available from http://newfirstsearch.oclc.org; Internet; accessed 25 May 2006.

Parents are to be the first and most important educators of their own children, diligently teaching them the Word of God. [See Deuteronomy 6:4-9.] Parents cannot franchise their responsibility to the congregation, no matter how faithful and biblical it may be. God assigned parents this non-negotiable responsibility, and children must see their Christian parents as teachers and fellow students of God's Word.[8]

Gelernter observes that college students are the driest timber he has ever come across because they know little or nothing about religion or Americanism because no one has ever bothered to give them anything spiritual that is worth having.[9] His comments underscore the real issue being, the lack of teaching in the home.

Burge has been involved in a recent study of the biblical and theological literacy of incoming freshmen at Wheaton College.[10] These students represent the evangelical church from all denominations and states. Most come from strong churches where there is a history of personal devotion and Christian involvement such as attendance, youth groups, camps, missions, etc. Burge gave the freshmen a 25-question test in which high-school groups averaged 50-55 percent correct. Burge confessed that many of these deficiencies also existed in the 1950s, which is also confirmed by the Gallup polls from that era, but argues that the baseline of minimally acceptable Bible knowledge has shifted. A summary of the test results gave a dramatic picture:

---

[8] Albert Mohler, "The Scandal of Biblical Illiteracy: It's Our Problem," available from http://crosswalk.com/news/weblogs/mohler/ ?adate=06/29/2004/; Internet; accessed 4 July 2006.

[9] Gelernter, "Bible Illiteracy in America," n.p.

[10] Gary Burge, "The Greatest Story Never Read. Our Biggest Challenge: Recovering Biblical Literacy in the Church." *Christianity Today* 43, no. 9, (August 9, 1999): 45-46 [journal on-line]; available from http://newfirstsearch.oclc.org; Internet; accessed 25 May 2006.

- Only 20% could place Moses, Adam, David, Solomon, or Abraham in chronological order.
- Only 15% could place in order the major events of Jesus' and Paul's lives.
- Only 20% knew that Acts was the place to look for Paul's travels.
- Only 60% could locate the Exodus story in the Old Testament.
- Only 33% could find the Sermon on the Mount in the New Testament.
- Only 20% cold find the Lord's Prayer.

There is also concern that biblical stories that have been made into cartoons are distorting the correct understanding of biblical truths for children. Turner, Jones, and Blazer maintain that after repeated showings of such biblical cartoon movies, the cartoons may so affect children's biblical understanding that the film images will predominate.[11] They add that these movies may overpower children's imaginations and suppress their ability to allow the biblical text to speak to them anew as they grow older. The authors conclude that the producers (and consequently, the parents), though well intentioned in providing a generation of children with Bible knowledge, may be fostering the worst kind of biblical ignorance.

Biblical Illiteracy in Christian Churches and Schools

There a number of church leaders who have voiced their concerns about the growing problem of biblical illiteracy in America. Note the following statements by some of these leaders.

---

[11] Helen Lee Turner, Amy E. Jones, and Doris A. Blazer, "The Hanna-Barbera Cartoons: Compounding Bible Ignorance?" *The Christian Century* 106 (March 1, 1989): 233-234 [journal on-line]; available from http://newfirstsearch.oclc.org; Internet; accessed 25 May 2006.

Note the comments of Christian sociologist George Barna from two of his survey updates:

> The Christian body in America is immersed in a crisis of biblical illiteracy. How else can you describe matters when most church-going adults reject the accuracy of the Bible, reject the existence of Satan, claim that Jesus sinned, see no need to evangelize, believe that good works are one of the keys to persuading God to forgive their sins, and describe their commitment to Christianity as moderate or even less firm?. . . In many ways, we are living in an age of theological anarchy.[12]

> While we cannot tell if the distinction in people's journey is due to life stage or to cultural shifts over time, it is obvious that people under 25 are substantially less likely to have undergone serious change because of time spent reading the Bible. With America already struggling from serious biblical illiteracy, the noticeable absence of the Bible in the lives of our youngest adults is likely to generate dramatic consequences in the decades to come.[13]

Wheaton professor of New Testament, Gary Burge adds the following from his essay:

> Obviously, we live in a postbiblical era where general knowledge of the Bible cannot be assumed. As a book, the Bible has been removed from their

---

[12] The Barna Group Ltd., "Religious Beliefs Vary Widely By Denomination," The Barna Update, June 25, 2001, available from http://www.barna.org/FlexPage.aspx?Page=BarnaUpdate&Barna UpdateID=92/; Internet; accessed 23 June 2006.
[13] The Barna Group, Ltd., "Half of Americans Say Faith Has "Greatly Transformed" Their Life," The Barna Update, June 6, 2006, available from http://www.barna.org/FlexPage.aspx?Page= BarnaUpdate&BarnaUpdateID=240/; Internet; accessed 23 June 2006.

reading lists of students so that they can barely recognize metaphors from great novels written before 1950. . . . We may lament the neglect of the Bible in popular culture and secular education, but we can understand it. But what about the church? What about the evangelical church? If it is true that biblical illiteracy is commonplace in secular culture at large, there is ample evidence that it points to similar trends in our churches.[14]

Woodrow Kroll, president of Back to the Bible quotes a lament from the renowned British missiologist Patrick Johnstone: "Christian donors need to be guided by the Lord rather than by their emotional response to physical suffering. The famine of the Word of God is still a more serious problem than that of food in Africa today."[15]

In a speech to Wheaton University, the Provost of Baylor University, David Jeffrey expressed his alarm at the biblical illiteracy and substandard orthodoxy in conservative Christian churches and at Baylor:

I am concerned that not only the wider culture, but increasingly the subculture we call the evangelical church has opinions on a book (the Bible) which, for practical intellectual purposes, it hasn't really read. . . . Even among more faithful faculty, biblical literacy and theological competence is at a far lower ebb than might have been found a generation ago amongst

---

[14] Gary Burge, "The Greatest Story Never Read," 45.

[15] Patrick Johnstone, *Operation World*, 21st Century Edition (Carlisle, England: Paternoster, 2001), 702; quoted in Woodrow Kroll, "Crisis in America," Bible Literacy Center, May 2004, available from http://www.bibleliteracycenter.com/articles/4/; Internet; accessed 25 May 2006.

rural Baptists and other evangelicals who never saw the inside of a college classroom.[16]

Biblical Illiteracy in Secular Schools

There are recent movements by the Bible Literacy Project (BLP) and the National Council on Bible Curriculum in Public Schools (NCBCPS) to advance the case for Bible literacy in the public schools across America (see Appendix A). There is some disagreement between the two organizations on how the Bible should be taught. Luke Timothy Johnson discusses the curriculum and textbooks of each organization, offering his evaluation of each.[17] Each organization has its own curriculum with the BLP using a standardized textbook titled, *The Bible and Its Influence*. The NCBCPS uses a textbook titled, *The Bible in History and Literature*. The main distinction between the two organizations is that that the BLP appears to be more of an ecumenical consortium of Christians and Jews while the NCBCPS is a conservative Christian effort.

The BLP argues that relatively few students receive high-quality academic instruction about the Old and New Testaments. When the heads of college English departments were asked what the single most important book is for an educated person to know at a minimum, their number one answer was the Bible.[18] The BLP further claims that students of

---

[16] Marv Knox, ed., "Baylor Provost's Speech Sparks Debate Over Baptist Freedom," *The Baptist Standard*, October 18, 2004, available from http://www.baptiststandard.com/postnuke/index.php?module=htmlpages&func=display&pid=2401/; Internet; accessed 24 July 2006.

17 Luke Timothy Johnson, "Textbook Case: A Bible Curriculum for Public Schools." *The Christian Century* 123, no. 4 (February 21, 2006): 34-37 [journal on-line]; available from http://newfirstsearch.oclc.org; Internet; accessed 2 July 2006.

18 Bible Literacy Project, "The Case for Bible Literacy in Secondary Schools," Bible Literacy Project, January 23, 2006, available from

all faiths need to know about the Bible to engage their American heritage in key areas of language, arts, and literature, as well as history, law, and politics. Without this Bible literacy, students are denied full access to their own linguistic, literary, and artistic heritage. The goal of the BLP is to study the Bible as literature and to understand the Bible's tremendous impact on the whole of Western tradition.[19]

Besides promoting consensus on the need for teaching about the Bible, another purpose of the BLP is to clear up the confusion about the Supreme Court decisions in the 1960s. The Supreme Court ruled that public schools may not require devotional use of the Bible, however, it explicitly acknowledged that academic study of the Bible in public schools is constitutional as part of a good education.[20] Many educators have failed to recognize this distinction and have simply stopped teaching about the Bible altogether.

---

http://www.bibleliteracy.org/Site/PressRoom/thecase.htm; Internet; accessed 26 May 2006.
[19] Ibid.
[20] Ibid.

CHAPTER 2

SIGNIFICANT BIBLE PASSAGES

Hosea 4:6

*"6 my people are destroyed from lack of knowledge. Because you have rejected knowledge, I also reject you as my priests; because you have ignored the law of your God, I also will ignore your children."*NIV

The concept of the knowledge of God is a major theological theme of the Old Testament book of Hosea.[21] The nation of Israel had turned its back on God and was guilty of apostasy. This was not a passive situation. God's case against Israel was that there was no faithfulness, no love and no acknowledgement of God. This was a willful rejection of God in the land. The key to the knowledge of God was obedience that came from the heart rather than burnt offerings that accompanied their idolatry to other gods (Hosea 6:6). Homer Hailey adds that the lack of knowledge was the stumbling block of the people and the priests were charged with "feeding on the sin of the people."[22] The priests were encouraging sin so they could prosper through sacrifices for sin.

Nichols argues that Hosea 4:6 and Isaiah 5:13 both show that this lack of knowledge was a result of rejecting what they already knew and that the problem was functional knowledge rather than cognitive awareness.[23] He points to the Pentateuch as evidence that the biblical thrust here in Hosea is on

---

[21] Robert D. Spender, "Theology of Hosea," n.p. in *Evangelical Dictionary of Biblical Theology*, [CD-ROM] (PC Study Bible Version 4.3C, Biblesoft, 1996).
[22] Homer Hailey, *A Commentary on the Minor Prophets* (Grand Rapids, Michigan: Baker Book House, 1972), 148.
[23] Nichols, "Communicating to a Biblically Illiterate World," 3.

functional knowledge or acting on what they already knew. However, the functional emphasis is still based upon knowing facts (one cannot act on what they do not know).

Isaiah 1:2-3; 5:12-13

"2 Hear, O heavens! Listen, O earth! For the LORD has spoken: I reared children and brought them up, but they have rebelled against me. 3 The ox knows his master, the donkey his owner's manger, but Israel does not know, my people do not understand." NIV

*"12 They have harps and lyres at their banquets, tambourines and flutes and wine, but they have no regard for the deeds of the LORD, no respect for the work of his hands. 13 Therefore my people will go into exile for lack of understanding; their men of rank will die of hunger and their masses will be parched with thirst."*NIV

The first chapter of Isaiah is probably an overview of God's oracles against Judah and Jerusalem. Isaiah speaks as Yahweh's lawyer, summoning the heavens and earth as witnesses to the Lord's claims and his right to bring charges against his people. The point here is that the great sin of Judah is spurning Yahweh's paternal love. This is a picture of the daily and intimate relationship that Judah enjoyed with God throughout her history. Nevertheless, here Isaiah is concerned with the rebellion of the people against God's law and against God personally. The parallelism in word pictures with animals is used to show that even animals are instinctively attracted to and are faithful to their masters. In contrast to these animals, God's people are uncaring and they live as if God had done nothing for them. The Hebrew word used here for rebelled indicates a breach of relationship. It implies apostasy—a deliberate act of turning away from God rather than an unknowing and passive ignorance. John Willis notes that the Hebrew verb translated **know** (*yadha'*) in 1:3 means to enjoy a personal, intimate, and trusting relationship.[24] In contrast to the animals, God's people do not know Yahweh and this is an unnatural, irresponsible, and illogical response. Both Nichols[25] and Hailey[26] are blunter in their evaluation of Isaiah's message that Judah is stupid compared to the ox and ass, which are not known for having high intelligence quotients.

Isaiah 5:12-13 is in the midst of a section of woes and threats announced by Yahweh. A woe is stronger in emphasis than a mere "shame on you." It is the expectation of severe punishment. The first woe in 5:8-10 is directed against the wicked rich who seize land from the poor as payment of debts. The second woe in 5:11-17 condemns the same wicked rich and all who adopt their thinking and lifestyle. The language in 5:12 is similar to Amos 6:4-6. The people are oblivious to the work of God in the world. They fail to acknowledge God's continual activity in nature, history, and human life because they are so preoccupied with their own interests. They will go into exile and die of hunger and thirst. Willis agrees with Nichols that their lack of knowledge does not mean ignorance as much as a failure to perceive the activity of God in the world.[27] Nichols argues that the "lack of knowledge" could be rendered as "without knowing it" meaning that Israel was blind to God's workings.[28] He reiterates that Isaiah here is concerned with functional illiteracy rather than cognitive literacy of God's word, meaning that they knew of God but refused to acknowledge him. Hailey adds that the lack of knowledge or understanding also implies that they were unaware that judgment and destruction was hanging over them.[29]

---

[24] John T. Willis, *Isaiah*, The Living Word Commentary on the Old Testament, ed. John T. Willis (Abilene, TX: ACU Press, 1984), 60-65.
[25] Nichols, "Communicating to a Biblically Illiterate World," 2.
[26] Homer Hailey, *A Commentary on Isaiah: With Emphasis on the Messianic Hope* (Grand Rapids, MI: Baker Book House, 1985), 38.
[27] Willis, "Isaiah," 132-133.
[28] Nichols, "Communicating to a Biblically Illiterate World," 2.
[29] Hailey, "A Commentary on Isaiah: With Emphasis on the Messianic Hope," 67.

Acts 17:30-31

"30 In the past God overlooked such ignorance, but now he commands all people everywhere to repent. 31 For he has set a day when he will judge the world with justice by the man he has appointed. He has given proof of this to all men by raising him from the dead." NIV

F. F. Bruce mentions that the coming of Christ marked a new beginning to how God deals with the human race.[30] In earlier times, people's ignorance of the knowledge of God was overlooked. When he fully revealed himself in the person of Jesus Christ, any subsequent ignorance is inexcusable. God no longer overlooks ignorance and Paul's statement is an imperative that all people everywhere is all-inclusive. I. H. Marshall suggests that we should draw a distinction between Paul's discussion in Romans 1:18ff about the way in which God gave up humankind to sin and its consequences, and the way in which he stresses the mercy of God who allows human ignorance when preaching the gospel to pagans.[31] No others who have heard the gospel can plead such ignorance.

In verse 31 Paul explains the purpose for the need to repent. In his sovereign counsel, God has fixed a day in which he will judge the world by the one who was incarnated and fully revealed his nature to the world. The proof of this future event, he says, is that God raised him from the dead. This is the resurrection hope that all Christians have because it is the proof of our own resurrection when Christ is revealed for the second time. Bruce adds that the knowledge of God set forth here by Paul is no mere philosophical discipline — it involves moral and religious responsibilities.[32] The hearers will be summoned to

---

[30] F. F. Bruce, *The Book of the Acts,* Revised ed. The New International Commentary on the New Testament, ed. Gordon Fee (Grand Rapids, Michigan: William B. Eerdmans Publishing Company, 1988), 340-342.
[31] I. H. Marshall, *The Book of Acts: An Introduction and Commentary,* The Tyndale New Testament Commentaries, ed. Leon Morris, vol. 5 (Grand Rapids, Michigan: William B. Eerdmans Publishing Company, 1980), 290.
[32] Bruce, *"The Book of the Acts,"* 341.

repentance in the measure in which this knowledge was accessible to them.

Hebrews 5:11-14

"11 We have much to say about this, but it is hard to explain because you are slow to learn. 12 In fact, though by this time you ought to be teachers, you need someone to teach you the elementary truths of God's word all over again. You need milk, not solid food! 13 Anyone who lives on milk, being still an infant, is not acquainted with the teaching about righteousness. 14 But solid food is for the mature, who by constant use have trained themselves to distinguish good from evil." NIV

In this passage, the Hebrew writer pauses long enough to address the practical issue of spiritual immaturity of his readers before resuming the discussion about Melchizedek. He is concerned that his Christian audience may not be able to grasp the importance of his message because they were slow learners (minds were sluggish) and therefore it will be hard to explain. He scolds them because they have been Christians for a long time and should be teachers by this time. Instead, they are still feeding on the milk of the Word rather than the solid food of mature grown-ups. They were unable to digest anything other than milk—the food of infants. Their "milk" corresponds to the ABCs of Christianity—the first principles which the author describes in Hebrews 6:1f (repentance, faith, baptisms, the laying on of hands, resurrection, and judgment). As infants of the Word, they were not able to distinguish between good and evil, right and wrong. This passage describes people who are biblically illiterate and ignorant. Unfortunately, many in our churches are still in this stage, having not graduated to mature status.

CHAPTER 3

A BRIEF SURVEY OF BIBLE ORIGINS, SIGNIFICANCE & LITERACY

Bible the Most Published and Printed Yet Misunderstood and Misinterpreted Book

The irony of the Bible is that it is the most published and printed book in history. Yet, by comparison, it is also the most misunderstood and misinterpreted book. To misunderstand and misinterpret by definition implies a certain degree of Bible literacy. By A.D. 500, the Bible had been translated into over 500 languages but by 600, it had been restricted to only one language: the Latin Vulgate.[33] For the next 800 years the Roman Catholic Church controlled Bible literacy via a campaign of forced ignorance. By 1400, men such as John Wycliffe and John Hus risked their lives to translate the Bible into the language of the people. With the invention of the printing press in 1453, the Bible was the first book to be printed on the printing press in 1455. There are only 22 complete Gutenberg Bibles in existence today with a value of $100 Million dollars each, should they ever come into the world market.[34] Other men such as William Tyndale, Desiderius Erasmus, and Martin Luther were instrumental in translating the Bible into English and German while inspiring the Protestant Reformation. Before Tyndale was burned at the stake for his efforts, he boldly told one official who criticized his efforts, "If God spare my life, I will see to it that the boy who drives the plowshare knows more of the

---

[33] Greatsite.com, "The Pre-reformation History of the Bible from 1,400 BC to 1,400 AD," Greatsite.com, 2003, available from http://www.greatsite.com/timeline-english-bible-history/pre-reformation.html; Internet; accessed 24 July 2006.

[34] Greatsite.com, "1455 Gutenberg Bible: The First Book Ever Printed," Greatsite.com, available from http://www.greatsite.com/facsimile-reproductions/gutenberg-1455.html; Internet; accessed 24 July 2006. These Gutenberg Bibles are the most valuable books in print today.

scripture than you, Sir!"[35] In a modern stark contrast to Tyndale, Woodrow Kroll remarked: "If Christians blew the dust off their Bibles at the same time, we'd all be killed in the dust storm."[36] The Bible had a profound influence on both British and American literature. Examples of the Bible's impact on the literature of authors such as John Milton, William Shakespeare, William Blake and others are countless. The history of the English Bible is a fascinating and sobering story that stands in sharp contrast to the value that Americans place on the reading and studying the Bible today.

Geneva Bible the Bible of Puritans, Pilgrims, and Protestant Reformation

The Geneva Bible was the first Bible taken to America, and became the Bible of the Puritans and Pilgrims. It is truly the "Bible of the Protestant Reformation."[37] David Gelernter tells the story of the importance of the Bible in the founding and development of Puritanism in England and then in America.[38] America was born in a passionate spiritual explosion that was created and fueled by the Bible. The Anglican and Puritan settlers came in search of religious freedom, to escape religious persecution in England, facts that Americans tend to forget. Gelernter adds that you cannot understand the literature and experience of 17th-century American pilgrims unless you know the Bible.[39] The Bible continued to shape American history. As the Civil War approached, the divided nation saw their struggle in biblical terms. Galernter quotes William Wolf that

---

[35] Greatsite.com, "English Bible History," Greatsite.com, available from http://www.greatsite.com/ timeline-english-bible-history/index.html; Internet; accessed 24 July 2006.

[36] Kroll, "Crisis in America," n.p.

[37] Ibid.

[38] David Gelernter, "Bible Illiteracy in America," *The Weekly Standard*, (May 23, 2005), available from http://www.weeklystandard.com/Content/Public/Articles/000/000/005/606lxblg.asp/; Internet; accessed 25 May 2006.

[39] Ibid.

Abraham Lincoln was America's most "biblical" president because no president had the detailed knowledge of the Bible that Lincoln had.[40]

The Bible Available to Virtually 99% of World's People

Because of Christian missions, the Bible has become available to virtually 99% of the world's people. In human history, this is unprecedented. It marks the greatest achievement in the history of communications.[41]

Bible Literacy Polls and Technology

In modern times as technology has allowed Bible literacy to be measured, George Gallup conducted a poll as far back as December 18, 1954 noting that only 1% of respondents could answer all ten questions of a Bible survey. Only 5% of respondents could answer nine of the ten questions while 4% could not answer a single question.[42] In a later poll conducted in 1990, the Gallup News Service concluded, "the Bible is still widely read and studied, but ignorance about its contents may be increasing."[43] In this poll, only half of adults could name one

---

[40] Ibid.

[41] W. Ritchey Hogg, "The Scriptures in the Christian World Mission: Three Historical Considerations," *Missiology* 12, no. 4 (October 1984): 399 [journal on-line]; available from http://newfirstsearch.oclc.org; Internet; accessed 2 July 2006.

[42] George Gallup, *How Well Do You Know the Bible?* (Princeton, NJ: Public Opinion News Service), American Institute of Public Opinion, 1, PDF, available from http://brain.gallup.com/Braincontent/release/1954_12_19.pdf; Internet; accessed 22 July 2006. This poll was claimed to be the first nationwide religion quiz among a representative sample of adults on 10 questions about the Bible and religion.

[43] George Gallup, Jr. and Frank Newport, *The Bible is Still Widely Read and Studied, But Biblical Illiteracy Remains Widespread* (Princeton, NJ: The Gallup Poll News Service), The Gallup Poll News Service, 55, No. 26a, 1, PDF, available from http://brain.gallup.com/Braincontent/release/1990_11_15.pdf; Internet; accessed 22 July 2006. This poll sample was a

of the four Gospels and only 37% in 1990, compared to 42% in 1982.[44] The Gallup Organization has since had numerous polls on biblical and religious knowledge in recent years with similar results.

telephone interview of 1000 randomly selected adults, 18 and older conducted on November 1-4, 1990.

[44] Ibid.

CHAPTER 4

SOME FACTORS THAT CAUSE BIBLICAL ILLITERACY

Only Half of Pastors and 9% of Adults Have a Biblical Worldview

The root cause of biblical illiteracy in the writer's view is that most people simply are not learning the Bible. However, the factors that contribute to that cause are complex and varied.

A disturbing trend noted by the Barna Group is that only half of our Protestant pastors (51%) have a biblical worldview.[45] Barna stated the following about these interviews:

> The low percentage of Christians who have a biblical worldview is a direct reflection of the fact that half of our primary religious teachers and leaders do not have one. In some denominations, the vast majority of clergy do not have a biblical worldview, and it shows up clearly in the data related to the theological views and moral choices of people who attend those churches. . . . The research also points out that even in churches where the pastor has a biblical worldview, . . . most of the congregants do not. More than six out of every seven congregants in the typical church do not share the biblical worldview of their pastor even when he or she has one. This intimates that merely preaching good sermons and offering helpful programs does not

---

[45] The Barna Group, Ltd., "Only Half of Protestant Pastors Have a Biblical Worldview," The Barna Update, January 12, 2004, available from http://www.barna.org/FlexPage.aspx?Page= BarnaUpdate&BarnaUpdateID=156/; Internet; accessed 25 May 2006.

enable most believers to develop a practical and scriptural theological base to shape their life. Our research among people who have a biblical worldview shows that it is a long-term process that requires a lot of purposeful activity: teaching, prayer, conversation, accountability, and so forth.[46]

In the same survey, Barna noted that only 9% of born again adults and 7% of Protestants possess a biblical worldview.[47] These may be surprising statistics but we can see biblical precedent for this phenomenon in the Bible itself. Isaiah 56:11 describes the shepherds of Judah and Jerusalem that cannot understand because they all turn to their own way, seeking their own gain. In Ezekiel 34 the prophet is directed to prophesy against the shepherds of Israel because they only took care of themselves. Obviously, part of caring for sheep is feeding them a nutritious diet of God's word. Note the following words of warning from the apostle Peter himself in 2 Peter 2:1-3:

> 1 But there were also false prophets among the people, just as there will be false teachers among you. They will secretly introduce destructive heresies, even denying the sovereign Lord who bought them—bringing swift destruction on themselves. 2 Many will follow their shameful ways and will bring the way of truth into disrepute. 3 In their greed these teachers will exploit you with stories they have made up. Their condemnation has long been hanging over them, and their destruction has not been sleeping. NIV

The sad commentary of Peter's prophecy is that this is happening today. We have so-called teachers in our churches and schools that deny the lordship and divinity of Jesus.

---

[46] Ibid.
[47] Ibid.

Members of groups such as the Jesus Seminar teach that the resurrection did not occur and that the Bible is only a human document. Consequently, they are destroying the faith of many and leading them astray.

Biblical Illiteracy, Theological Heterodoxy, and Moral Frailty

Woodrow Kroll maintains that the result of Bible illiteracy is theological heterodoxy (whacky theology).[48] He further argues that theological heterodoxy always leads to moral frailty. He cites the following research to make his point:

- Less than .5% of those with a biblical worldview said voluntary exposure to pornography was morally acceptable (compared to 39% of other adults).

- People with a biblical worldview were eight times less likely to buy lottery tickets and 17 times less likely to place bets than those without a biblical worldview.

- One out eight adults with a secular worldview had sexual relations with someone other than their spouse during the last month. Less than 1% of individuals with a biblical worldview had done so.

Pastors and Teachers Must Contextualize in a Post-Christian Postmodern Era

Robert Coleman stated, "Evangelists in Western Culture who fail to contextualize, with the knowledge that we are in a post-Christian era, will find themselves communicating to

---

[48] Woodrow Kroll, "All Christians Have a Biblical Worldview, Right?" Bible Literacy Center, available from http://www.bibleliteracycenter.com/page_print.php?link=/articles/6/; Internet; accessed 25 May 2006.

fewer and fewer people."[49] Coleman rightly observes that we must contextualize the message for the audience without compromising the truth. In recent years, we have gained knowledge of learning theory and how it should be applied to fit the audience. The use of different technologies has also improved how that knowledge is presented. It seems that many teachers in this post-Christian postmodern era have not learned these principles yet and there is resistance to learning them.

Nichols also presents a similar factor in citing Lesslie Newbigin who observed that the present society has turned to a type of post-Christian paganism that was born out of the rejection of Christianity and is far more resistant to the gospel than pre-Christian paganism, which is more familiar to cross-cultural missions.[50]

Information Overload and Biblical Illiteracy

Nichols discusses our information overload society as another factor that contributes to biblical illiteracy. He cites research that we receive from 15,000 to 18,000 messages a week but can only process 700-800 messages effectively.[51] Thus, we have knowledge coming at a faster rate than we can receive it. Nichols wrote this essay just prior to the invention of the internet so the problem of information overload and processing has compounded exponentially in the last decade.

Being Relevant, Situation Ethics, and Biblical Illiteracy

Daniel describes some dynamics within churches that reveal other factors.[52] She describes a church she was raised in where the Sunday school was small and unimaginative. Her

---

[49] Robert Coleman, *Evangelism on the Cutting Edge* (Old Tappan, NJ: Fleming H. Revell, 1986), 82; quoted in Nichols, "Communicating to a Biblically Illiterate World," 5-6.

[50] Ibid., 6.

[51] Nichols, "Communicating to a Biblically Illiterate World," 4-5.

[52] Daniel, "I Love to Tell the Story to Those Who Know It Least," 49-50.

teacher told them to draw the baby Jesus every week and create a puppet of him. Her Jesus was more cute than compelling. In another church, Daniel related that Sunday school teachers were encouraged to be relevant. Instead of reading Bible stories, they did situation ethics. Daniel describes it this way:

> Lifeboat dilemmas and debates on the Cold War took the place of Scripture memorization. When Jesus made an appearance in these debates, we tended to imagine him carrying a guitar. We learned a lot about how we felt but little about the God who created us. Raised in the church in an age of cultural relativism, some end up like a football player who graduated from high school without learning to read, sent out into the world biblically illiterate.[53]

The Diminishing Role of Biblical Preaching and Teaching in Churches

Mohler cites the diminishing role of biblical preaching and teaching in our churches as another contributing factor.[54] Churches have marginalized biblical knowledge and Bible teaching accounts for a diminishing fraction of church time and attention. Sound expository biblical preaching has taken a back seat to other concerns in corporate worship.

The Failure of the Church to Transmit Religious Culture to Next Generation

Burge echoes Mohler's sentiments that there is a general failing of the church to transmit our religious culture to the next generation. He says this includes an overemphasis on personal experience to the neglect of education and instruction. Sermons have become more therapeutic and less instructional. It is more

---

[53] Ibid., 50.
[54] Mohler, "The Scandal of Biblical Illiteracy: It's Our Problem," n.p.

valid on Sundays to be grounded in how we feel rather than what we think. Christian churches have abandoned serious Bible exposition and theological teaching so that historical exegesis is becoming a "lost art" in the pulpit. Preachers are taking biblical passages out of context in order to evoke the emotional responses or desired attitudes of their audience.[55]

The Influence of Unbiblical Philosophies and Worldviews on Biblical Illiteracy

Michael Vlach, founder and president of TheologicalStudies.org discusses the tremendous influence that unbiblical philosophies and worldviews are as contributing factors to biblical and theological illiteracy.[56] Liberalism promotes the Bible as a human document. Existentialism and humanism emphasize human experience as the ultimate self-help programs. Postmodernism has convinced many that there are no universal truths or absolute moral truth. The danger in succumbing to these influences is that biblically illiterate Christians are embracing and adopting elements of these secular human philosophies and religious teachings of other world religions and even cult systems into their faith without even knowing it. This phenomenon is known as syncretism or religious pluralism. The evidence for correlating religious pluralism with biblical illiteracy needs to be an area for further research.

---

[55] Burge, "The Greatest Story Never Read," 47-48.

[56] Michael Vlach, "Crisis in America's Churches: Bible Knowledge at All-time Low," TheologicalStudies.org, n.p, available from http://www.theologicalstudies.citymax.com/page/page/573625.htm; Internet; accessed 4 July 2006.

CHAPTER 5

SOME CONSEQUENCES OF BIBLICAL ILLITERACY

Perfect Candidates for Cults, Human Philosophies, and World Religions

Edward Dalcour reminds us that the by-product of those in our churches who are biblically illiterate makes them perfect candidates for non-Christian cults, human philosophies, and other world religions.[57] He argues that illiterate Christians lack doctrinal discernment and consequently, cannot demonstrate biblically the natures of God and Christ. It is paramount that Christians learn to communicate the person of Christ. A recent Barna Group survey of biblical beliefs by denomination showed what described as a remarkable insight into America's faith—that less than half of all adults (40%) are convinced that Jesus Christ lived a sinless life during his time on earth.[58] Dalcour cites 2 Peter 3:16 to show that the ignorant (*amatheis*) people in that passage literally means *unstudied* or *untrained*.[59] When people are untrained, they distort Scripture and Peter says the consequence of that distortion is their destruction (note Hosea 4:6).

---

[57] Edward Dalcour, "The Biblical Illiteracy in the Christian Church," Reformation Online, available from
http://www.reformationonline.com/illiteracy.htm; Internet; accessed 29 June 2006.
[58] The Barna Group, Ltd., "Religious Beliefs Vary Widely By Denomination," n.p.
[59] Ibid.

The Biblically Illiterate are Silent in the Face of Evil or Error

Both Dalcour[60] and Daniel[61] note that when people are biblically illiterate they tend to be silent in the face of evil or error. In all fairness, this is not always due to ignorance — it can be due to a lack of courage to confront. In today's contemporary culture, it is easy to side with the majority who advocate tolerance. Many sincere Christians may do this because they do not want to be guilty of judging. In contrast, Dalcour adds that it is the biblical responsibility of Christians to judge actions and doctrine even though we cannot judge motives (note Paul's direction on this in 1 Corinthians 5:12 and Titus 1:9). Christians cannot "contend for the faith" (Jude 3) if they are illiterate about that faith. Daniel tells of noting adults in her congregation who will not teach Sunday school because they feel illiterate. A consequence of this illiteracy is shame and embarrassment because they confess that they know less than their children about the Bible.

Women Traditionally the Spiritual Leaders, Mentors, and Role Models

The Barna Group recently noted in a nationwide survey that women are 29% more likely to read the Bible than men.[62] Consequently, women more likely to take on the role of spiritual leader, mentor, and role model in the family. Note Barna's assessment in this area:

> If the Church is to stem the tide of biblical illiteracy and waning commitment to the Christian faith, men will have to reestablish themselves as partners and leaders of the spiritual functions of families. . . . The

---

[60] Dalcour, "The Biblical Illiteracy in the Christian Church," n.p.

[61] Daniel, "I Love to Tell the Story to Those Who Know it Least," 49.

[62] The Barna Group, Ltd., "Women are the Backbone of the Christian Congregations in America," The Barna Update, March 6, 2000, available from http://www.barna.org/FlexPage.aspx?Page=BarnaUpdate&BarnaUpdateID=47/; Internet; accessed 23 June 2006.

apparent lack of spiritual leadership exhibited by millions of Christian men has significantly hampered the spiritual growth of tens of thousands of well-meaning but spiritually inert families.[63]

Biblically Illiterate Men Lack Spiritual Leadership

Organizations such as Promise Keepers are encouraging men to be more responsible spiritual leaders but more improvement is needed. Barna noted that a consequence of the heavier load that women bear in this area is taking its toll in burnout with a corresponding decline in attendance (22%) and volunteer work (21%).[64] A study by Robert Ortiz and Laurie McCarty has shown that the involvement of fathers in the education of their children is a crucial component in the classroom.[65] Though this study focused primarily on the secular literacy of children, the principles are germane to family Bible Study and Sunday school literacy in the church. It is frightening trend that in a recent nationwide survey on Bible reading, Barna noted that Mosaics (the generation of individuals born between 1984-2002) were particularly resistant to the Bible.[66] Mosaics were 24% less likely to read the Bible than Baby Busters (the generation of individuals born between 1965 and 1983).[67]

Biblical Illiteracy Poisons Individuals, Churches, and Communities

Mark Copeland concludes that biblical illiteracy is like a poison, wreaking havoc in the lives of individuals, in our

---

[63] Ibid.

[64] Ibid.

[65] Robert W. Ortiz and Laurie L. McCarty, ""Daddy, Read to Me": Fathers Helping Their Young Children Learn to Read." *Reading Horizons* 38 (November/December 1997): 108-115 [journal on-line]; available from http://newfirstsearch.oclc.org; Internet; accessed 2 July 2006.

[66] George Barna, *The State of the Church: 2006* (Ventura, CA: The Barna Group, Ltd), 34.

[67] Ibid., 52.

churches, and in our communities. He evaluates the consequences with the following questions:

> How many lives are being destroyed, how many people are stumbling through life, because they do not have the light of God's word guiding them? . . . How many churches are "dying on the vine," or into wholesale apostasy because their members cannot discern between truth and error? . . . Consider how the moral fabric of our nation and others in the world are becoming unraveled when "everyone does what is right in his own eyes" - Judges 21:25. [68]

Bible Ignorance Perpetuated By Distorted Cartoons and Movies

A consequence of Bible ignorance noted by Turner, Jones, and Blazer is that Hanna-Barbera and other cartoons based upon Bible stories may overpower children's imaginations and suppress their ability to allow the biblical text to speak to them anew as they grow older.[69] Their study of these cartoons noted that Hanna-Barbera portrays the heroes as so mighty and good that they overshadow God. After repeatedly watching these cartoons, the biblical understanding of these children may so affected that the film images will predominate in their perception of the biblical stories. Cartoons do not have a monopoly on this issue. Adult movies may have the same affect upon biblically illiterate adults.

---

[68] Mark A. Copeland, "Biblical Illiteracy," Executable Outlines, available from http://www.ccel.org/ contrib/exec_outlines/top/bibillit.htm; Internet; accessed 25 May 2006.

[69] Turner, Jones, and Blazer, "The Hanna-Barbera Cartoons: Compounding Bible Ignorance?" 233.

CHAPTER 6

SUMMARY AND CONCLUSIONS

Summary

In summary, this book was an investigation of the systemic problem of biblical illiteracy in American families, churches, and schools. The research was primarily religious in nature and most data are from Christian sources but some data from secular schools and polls was given. Definitions for Bible literacy and biblical illiteracy were given but they are derived from testing and observation from pastoral staff, as there are no standard official definitions. Several Bible passages from the Old and New Testaments that demonstrated the nature of biblical illiteracy among God's people were evaluated and discussed. A brief survey of Bible origins, significance, and literacy was provided for background information on the importance of the Bible and its place in history. Some factors that cause biblical illiteracy from different sources were discussed to determine where the problems are found. Finally, some consequences of biblical illiteracy from different experts in pastoral and educational fields were examined and evaluated. Some recommended solutions for biblical illiteracy were included as Appendix A rather than in the main body due to the limits of this paper. Organizations that sponsor and promote Bible literacy were included in Appendix B to facilitate readers who might need resources about this topic. The spiritual decision-making model of James Engle was added as Appendix C because of its usefulness in viewing the communication and understanding of the dynamics of where people are in their decision-making process.

Conclusions

Barna Research Shows Recent Hopeful Trends Without Transition in Beliefs

In their State of the Church report for 2006, the Barna Group notes some recent hopeful trends tempered with a dose of caution.[70] Their tracking data for 2006 indicates, "God is hot" now resulting in observable behavioral change without much transition evident in beliefs. Barna says this distinction is critical because lasting change comes only when beliefs are altered. He argues that if there is change without change in the underlying core beliefs, it will be temporary because the past research has shown that the behavior eventually reverts back to its original state.

Barna Encouraged by Decade of Increased Religious Behaviors

Barna is also encouraged by the increases in the number of religious behaviors in the past decade such as Bible reading, church attendance, small group involvement, Sunday school attendance, and volunteerism.[71] He also noted in a recent Barna Update that people who read the Bible regularly were more than twice as likely as those who do not to have undergone faith-based transformation.[72] However, he again urges caution suggesting there may not be a real corresponding movement in people's beliefs that transforms their relationships with God. He is optimistic that there will be some permanent transitions in beliefs with the upsurge over the last 10 years in Bible reading and other commitments to spiritual growth and service.

---

[70] The Barna Group, Ltd., "The State of the Church: 2006," 50.
[71] Ibid.
[72] The Barna Group, Ltd. "Half of Americans Say Faith Has "Greatly Transformed" Their Life," n.p.

Bible Literates Will Never Dominate the Church

Lillian Daniel takes the rational approach that as we spend more time with the Bible and those in our communities grow more familiar with the Word, it will be tempting to assume a growing literacy.[73] However, those who are Bible literate will never dominate the church and we must always make room for the obvious questions. Daniel reminds us that as today's preachers bemoan biblical illiteracy, we would do well to remember the time when believers were not allowed to read God's Word for themselves at all. The other side of that thought, however, is that we have resources and tools available to us today like no other time in history. There are no excuses for not searching out and finding materials for sound Bible study. As Jesus' sobering words remind us in Luke 12:48, "But the one who does not know and does things deserving punishment will be beaten with few blows. From everyone who has been given much, much will be demanded; and from the one who has been entrusted with much, much more will be asked (NIV)."

The Problem of Biblical Illiteracy Will Never Disappear

The problem of biblical illiteracy in this country will never disappear. Both the Scriptures and history bear witness that fact. Research from institutions such as the Gallup Organization and The Barna Group are useful in identifying and tracking trends. It is clear that biblical illiteracy is rampant in our families, churches, and schools where the teaching of the Bible should be occurring. Many people are predicting dire consequences for our families and churches. Only time will tell and only God knows how extensive and pervasive the problem really is. An area for future research is to investigate the possible correlation between biblical illiteracy and religious pluralism.

---

[73] Daniel, "I Love to Tell the Story to Those Who Know it Least," 50.

APPENDIX A

SOME RECOMMENDED SOLUTIONS FOR BIBLICAL ILLITERACY

Bible Literary Requires Reinforcement and Repetition

Many ministers do not have the luxury of teaching a biblically literate church. Lillian Daniel explains that it is helpful for her to provide an introduction to every story.[74] She goes in depth with one passage, always retelling the story. Her goal with every sermon is for those who hear it to remember which passage was preached on. For Daniel, the issue here appears to be reinforcement and repetition rather than jumping from passage to passage like many preachers tend to do in expository sermons.

Congregational Leadership Must Make Biblical Illiteracy Top Priority

Harold Percy offers the following solutions for biblical illiteracy: [75]

1. *This needs to be a top priority for anyone in congregational leadership.* The goal of discipleship is not simply biblical knowledge but changed lives. However, we cannot make disciples without helping them to become biblically literate.

---

[74] Daniel, "I Love to Tell the Story to Those Who Know it Least," 50.

[75] Harold Percy, "The Scandal of Biblical Illiteracy," *Ministry Matters*, January 19, 2004, available from http://generalsynod.anglican.ca/ministries/departments/mm/2004/winter/mm17.html; Internet; accessed 18 July 2006.

2. *Addressing this problem requires starting at the beginning.* The Bible is a collection of books with many different types of literature, written against all kinds of backgrounds and in all kinds of contexts. The need here is to be proactive and creative in finding ways to give people an overview of the Bible. This includes understanding of where it came from, how it is arranged, and the social and historical contexts. Leaders must provide meaningful help in how to read the Bible for understanding, guidance, nourishment, and spiritual growth.

Congregational leaders who make this a priority and are willing to work hard will be richly rewarded. The people are eager for this and they have the right to expect it. The congregational atmosphere will be transformed with new levels of excitement, anticipation, and commitment.

Bible Reading, Study, Parents, Preachers the Antidote to Biblical Illiteracy

Mark Copeland offers the following antidote to biblical illiteracy:[76]

1. *Daily devotional Bible reading in private.* Are you willing to do your part, every day, in stamping out biblical illiteracy?

2. *Frequent in-depth Bible study with others.* Are you willing to participate in such activities to stamp out biblical illiteracy?

3. *Parents accepting their God-given responsibilities.* Are you willing to accept your parental duties to stamp out biblical illiteracy?

---

[76] Mark A. Copeland, "Biblical Illiteracy," n.p.

4. *Preachers fulfilling their duty to the Word.* Are you willing to require that preachers proclaim the Word to stamp out biblical illiteracy?

Voluntary, Informal Bible Study Better Predictor of Biblical Knowledge

A recent study by Robert Filback and Stephen Krashen investigated the impact of voluntary reading of the Bible, comparing its effect to other possible predictors and controlling for some possible confounds.[77] The purpose of their study was to determine whether pleasure reading of the Bible resulted in significant biblical knowledge compared to formal study. Their study concluded that voluntary reading of the Bible was a good predictor of biblical knowledge. Those who enjoy reading the Bible more, who say they read it more, and who engage in more informal study have superior knowledge of the Bible. The results were overwhelmingly in favor of voluntary reading and informal study. Those who study on their own are more able to pursue special interests.

Study Shows Correlation Between Church Position and Education Level

Another older study by Jerry Willis did not see any significant increase in Bible knowledge when church members were exposed to the educational programs and sermons of the church.[78] There was a lack of significant correlations between biblical knowledge and factors such as age, number of years a church member, and attendance for children and adolescents.

---

[77] Robert Filback and Stephen Krashen, "The Impact of Reading the Bible and Studying the Bible on Biblical Knowledge." Knowledge Quest: *Journal of the American Association of School Librarians* 31, no. 2 (November/December 2002): 50-51 [journal on-line]; available from http://newfirstsearch.oclc.org; Internet; accessed 25 May 2006.

[78] Jerry Willis, "Correlates of Bible Knowledge." *Journal for the Scientific Study of Religion* 7 (Fall 1968): 280-281 [journal on-line]; available from http://newfirstsearch.oclc.org; Internet; accessed 25 May 2006.

There were only two factors that were found to correlate with Biblical knowledge: the position held in church and the education level.

Leaders Must Diagnose Problems, Reconstruct Educational Ministry, Identify Teachers

Gary Burge has hope that the church should not despair regarding biblical illiteracy. He mentions that new ministries to men such as Promise Keepers and other strategic creative ministries to young people are emerging to take on the problem. Burge offers the following strategies to address the problem of biblical illiteracy:[79]

1. *The first step must be diagnosis.* Leaders must assess the true condition of their sheep before feeding them. Developing a simple questionnaire will give unparalleled insight into the strengths and weaknesses of the people.

2. *We must reconstruct the educational ministry for the church.* Adult education ministers can develop core classes such as Old Testament Survey, New Testament Survey, Christian Doctrines, and Christian Disciplines that are offered on a rotating basis.

3. *Parachurch ministries such as Bible Study Fellowship are another strategy to supplement the educational curriculum.*

4. *We need to be alert to the educational dimension of the church's sermons.* Repetition and replowing familiar ground will reinforce learning.

5. *We need to identify young men and women in the church who are gifted in teaching and intellect and encourage and equip them to pursue their gifts.* Rediscovering the teaching pastor is a desperately needed vocation.

---

[79] Burge, "The Greatest Story Never Read," 48-49.

Establish Bible Electives in High School — College Students Next Great Awakening

David Gelernter offers the following solutions to biblical illiteracy in the schools:[80]

1. *Every School that teaches history must teach the Bible's central role.* High school history and English curricula should be rebuilt from scratch to teach students about the centrality of the Bible.

2. *Students need to read the Bible — not just about the Bible.* Bible as literature electives should be developed that keep clear of teaching the Bible as a sacred text that promotes religious views. Such courses should also include the bleak history of Bible teaching that refuses to teach the Bible as sacred literature. These courses should be offered in every public high school.

3. *It is impossible to find the one global solution to the problem of Bible teaching in America.* However, the one global hope is that America is fertile ground for Great Awakenings where mass movements of the population return to their religious roots. America is overdue for such an event that will probably be centered in the Protestant community in friendship with other religious communities.

4. *The next Great Awakening will happen among college students.* They are empty — spiritually bone dry — because no one has ever bothered to give them anything spiritual that is worth having. If the right person speaks to them, they will turn back to the Bible with an excitement and exhilaration that will shake the country.

---

[80] Gelernter, "Bible Illiteracy in America," n.p.

Churches Must Recover Centrality and Urgency of Biblical Teaching and Preaching

Albert Mohler offers the solution that churches must recover the centrality and urgency of biblical teaching and preaching, while refusing to sideline the teaching ministry of the preacher.[81] We will not believe more than we know and we will not live higher than our beliefs.

Churches Must Use Revelation/Response Education, Presence/Presentation Evangelism

Charles Nichols offers the following solutions in communicating to biblically illiterate people:[82]

1. *Use Revelation/Response Education.* The church needs to move from the informational model (concrete sequential approach) to the revelation/response model. People are learning facts but see no relevance in real life. Revelation/response teaching aims at presenting content in correlation to life and relationships. It affirms the role of Scripture in the process while allowing for the activity of the Holy Spirit to work through spiritual mentors and the faith community at large to promote the internal spiritual transformation required in Romans 8:29 and 12:2.

2. *Use Presence/Presentation Evangelism.* The church needs to move from the entrepreneurial model to the presence/presentation model as noted by Jesus in Matthew 5:16. This necessitates a presence and a witness among people. It also demands people in relationship presenting truth in clear, correct ways. These components require biblically literate Christians who are living their faith and are able to articulate the message to others. Nichols

---

[81] Mohler, "The Scandal of Biblical Illiteracy: It's Our Problem," n.p.
[82] Nichols, "Communicating to a Biblically Illiterate World," 7-11.

advocates using the Engle model of decision-making in communicating the gospel (note this model in Appendix B).

Churches Must Affirm Authority of God's Word, Read Bible With Expectancy, Model

Missiologist Howard Culbertson suggests the following strategies for churches to reverse the rising tide of biblical illiteracy:[83]

1. *Affirm the authority of God's Word.* We claim to believe that the Bible is the primary source of truth. While other "teachers" may include life experiences, reason, and church history, we must never accord these sources the same level of authority as God's Word.

2. *Read the Bible with a sense of expectancy.* Many times biblical passages are heard without reverent ears so many times that they can be read without engaging the mind. The Word disintegrates into merely words. Every time we read Scripture, we should sense that a new insight or new idea might be waiting for us. Even when reading familiar and well read passages, growing Christians should come to God's Word seeking fresh understandings of God's revelation.

3. *Directly encounter the Word.* Bible study can be done two ways: inductively or deductively. Deductive Bible study begins with a life situation, a problem, or a decision and work back to the Bible for examples, answers, and guidance. Inductive Bible study also starts with a biblical passage, and discovers life truths using the investigative tools at hand. Both methods are helpful; however, the deductive method often becomes overused because it appears to be "easier"

---

[83] Howard Culbertson, "Why Johnny Can't Read . . . the Bible," Southern Nazarene *University,* http://home.snu.edu/~hculbert/flesch.htm; Internet; accessed 29 June 2006.

and perhaps more immediately helpful. Inductive Bible study allows the Word to "speak for itself," and should regularly be used by adults.

4. *Encourage Bible study dialogue.* This is dialogue in which believers can enrich each other's understanding of God's Word.

5. *Model for other believers the effectiveness of Bible principles.* The Bible is not an ancient, boring document that is unrelated to life. It is a book about life today and every passage speaks of life. Christians can and should take every opportunity to talk about how regular Bible study does make a real difference in the way we live.

6. *Promote Bible study tools.* In most cases, we can go directly to God's Word and understand it. Bible study aids such as commentaries, Bible dictionaries and Bible handbooks can deepen our understanding. Acts 8 tells the story of an Ethiopian reading from Isaiah without fully understanding what he was reading. Many adults find themselves frustrated in similar ways in their Bible reading. Mature Christians can help them find keys to unlocking the Word just as Philip did with that Ethiopian.

Marlowe's Ten Steps to Biblical Literacy

Michael Marlowe has the following abbreviated ten steps to biblical literacy:[84]

1. *Choose a dynamic equivalent or essentially literal Bible translation.* Recommended versions are the English Standard Version, New American Standard Bible, New

---

[84] Michael Marlow, "Ten Steps to Biblical Literacy," Bible Research, available from http://www.bible-researcher.com/bible-study2.html; Internet; accessed 29 June 2006.

King James Version, or the New International Version. Choose a translation for which you can get audio tapes or CDs. Get an edition of the version that has the translators' notes and plenty of cross-references. Do not use a cheap edition that omits these notes and cross-references. The book and tapes will cost you about $150, but it will certainly be one of the best investments of your life.

2. *Listen to the entire Bible on tape three times over a period of six months.* Listen to an entire book at one sitting

3. *Listen to the tape of Paul's epistle to the Romans while following along in your Bible.* Do the entire epistle in one sitting.

4. *Read the epistle to the Romans again without the tape.* Do the whole book at one sitting.

5. *Read the epistle to the Romans again while looking up the first cross-reference in every chapter.* Put a question mark next to any verse you do not understand and continue reading.

6. *Read the epistle again (including notes), this time looking up any cross-references given in the places where you put a question mark before*

7. *Begin a daily routine of reading one of the Psalms, pray to God for understanding of his Word, and ready at least three chapters of the New Testament*

8. *Read the Old Testament from the beginning, proceeding in the same manner as outlined above*

9. *Read the New Testament again.* You will be amazed at how much more you get out of the New Testament the second time, after having read the Old Testament

10. *Obtain an inexpensive commentary such as Matthew Henry, Albert Barnes, or Jamieson, Fausset, and Brown.* Then go

through your Bible and find all those question marks you have made in the margins, and see what the commentator has to say about the passages.

This entire process should take about three years, after which you will probably be among the more biblically literate in your congregation. Consequently, you will feel confident in offering comments at Bible study meetings.

Leaders Must Acknowledge, Evaluate, Instruct, Alert, Encourage

Michael Vlach has the following solutions from his thoughtful essay:[85]

1. *Church leaders need to be aware of the crisis.* They must first acknowledge that we are in a state of spiritual chaos. The problem with many leaders is they refuse to believe the possibility that this is the case. Many unfortunately have the ostrich-head-in-the-sand syndrome.

2. *Pastors and church leaders need to evaluate what their people know and believe.* This interaction with the congregation would involve using doctrinal questionnaires and Bible literacy tests to find out what people know and believe. It can no longer be assumed that the people in the pews know the basics. The results of such tests will reveal what the strengths and weakness are so that a strategy of educating in these areas could be developed.

3. *Church leaders must use powerful ways to instruct their people in the truth.* They need to adopt new approaches to educating people about God's word and new tools to facilitate growth. This would include a well-planned

---

[85] Vlach, "Crisis in America's Churches: Bible Knowledge at All-Time Low," n.p.

systematic approach to biblical truth. Church members should be introduced to basic courses in Old Testament Survey, New Testament Survey, Basic Christian Doctrines, and How to Study the Bible. Pastors and ministers learn these basics in seminary or Bible college but are not transmitting them to the people in the pews. Thus, a large gap exists between what is being taught in seminaries and what is being taught in our churches.

4. *Church leaders, including pastors, must alert their members to the unbiblical worldviews and philosophies that have crept into the church.* False teachings have infiltrated the church and leaders must take proactive steps to confront these errors.

5. *We must encourage diligent and gifted teachers in the church.* This requires identifying young men and women in the church who are gifted in teaching and encourage them to pursue and use these gifts.

APPENDIX B

ORGANIZATIONS THAT PROMOTE BIBLE LITERACY PROGRAMS

Bible Literacy Project

- <u>Website</u>: http://www.bibleliteracy.org/Site/index2.htm

- <u>Mission</u>: The Bible Literacy Project, Inc. is a non-partisan, non-profit endeavor to encourage and facilitate the academic study of the Bible in public schools. Founded in 2001 by Chuck Stetson, we believe that failure to teach about the Bible leaves students in ignorance and cultural illiteracy.

- <u>Contact Info</u>

  Bible Literacy Project
  122 W. 14th Street PMB 332
  Front Royal, VA 22630
  Phone: 540-622-2265
  Fax: 866-214-1147
  Email: info@bibleliteracy.org

National Council on Bible Curriculum in Public Schools

- <u>Website</u>: http://www.bibleinschools.net/sdm.asp

- <u>Mission</u>: This is to bring a state certified Bible course (elective) into the public high schools nationwide. The curriculum for the program shows a concern to convey the content of the Bible as compared to literature and history. The program is concerned with education rather than indoctrination of students. The central approach of the class is simply to study the Bible as a foundation document of society, and that approach is altogether appropriate in a comprehensive program of secular education.

- Contact Info:

  National Council On Bible Curriculum In Public Schools
  Post Office Box 9743
  Greensboro, North Carolina 27429
  Toll Free: (877) OnBible
  Phone: (336) 272-3799
  Fax: (336) 272-7199

The Bible Literacy Center

- Website: http://www.bibleliteracycenter.com/

- Mission: Believing that only God's inspired Word changes peoples' lives, the mission of the Bible Literacy Center (BLC) is to stimulate meaningful Bible reading and Bible study that will equip the reader with a biblical worldview, biblical answers to life's questions, and a biblical lifestyle that will "present everyone complete in Christ Jesus" (Colossians 1:29).

- Contact Info

  The Bible Literacy Center
  P.O. Box 82808
  Lincoln, NE 68501
  Phone: 1-800-769-6655
  E-mail: info@bibleliteracycenter.com

Back to the Bible

- Website: http://www.backtothebible.org/

- <u>Mission</u>: Back to the Bible is a worldwide Christian ministry dedicated to leading people into a dynamic relationship with God. Using radio, the Internet, TV and other media, we share the Gospel message and help Christians grow to spiritual maturity. With broadcasts in more than 25 languages and an Internet reach to millions, Back to the Bible teaches the Word and touches the world.

- <u>Contact Info</u>:

Back to the Bible
P.O. Box 82808
6400 Cornhusker Highway
Lincoln, NE 68501-2808, USA
Toll Free: 800-811-2397
Phone: 402-464-7200
Fax: 402-464-7474
Email: info@backtothebible.org

APPENDIX C

JAMES ENGLE SPIRITUAL DECISION-MAKING MODEL

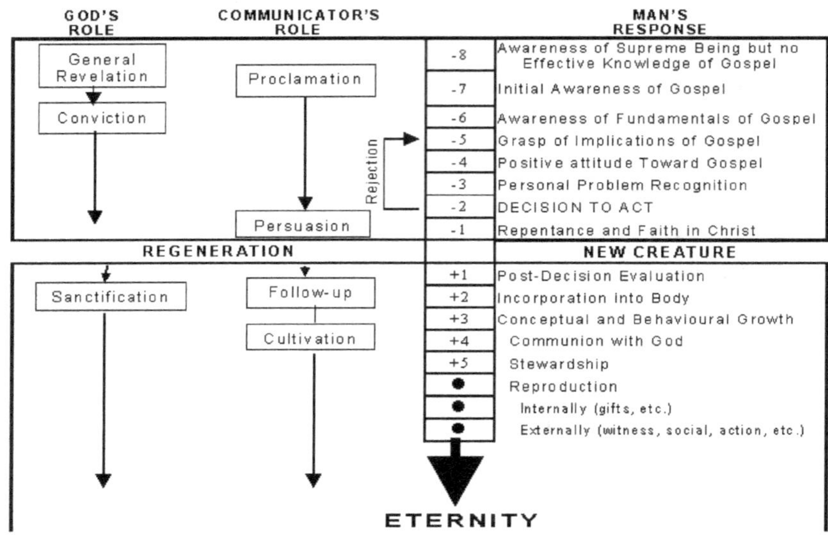

James Engel is director of the Billy Graham graduate program in communications at the Wheaton College Graduate School. This model depicts the roles of God, the communicator and the listener in the process of communicating the gospel. Everyone we talk to falls somewhere on this scale in terms of his spiritual decision-making process and receptivity to the gospel.[86]

---

[86] Web Evangelism Guide, "An Interpersonal Communication Model: The Engle Scale Explained," *Gospelcom.net*, available from http://guide.gospelcom.net/resources/tellitoften.php/; Internet; accessed 29 July 2006.

WORKS CITED

Bible Literacy Project. "The Case for Bible Literacy in
     Secondary Schools." Bible Literacy Project, January 23,
     2006. http://www.bibleliteracy.org/Site/PressRoom/
     thecase.htm; Internet; accessed 26 May 2006.

Bruce, F. F. *The Book of the Acts, Revised ed.* The New
     International Commentary on the New Testament, ed.
     Gordon Fee. Grand Rapids, Michigan: William B.
     Eerdmans Publishing Company, 1988.

Burge, Gary M. "The Greatest Story Never Read. Our Biggest
     Challenge: Recovering Biblical Literacy in the Church."
     Christianity Today 43, no. 9, (August 9, 1999): 45-49
     [journal on-line]; available from OCLC FirstSearch
     ArticleFirst Database, http://newfirstsearch.oclc.org;
     Internet; accessed 25 May 2006.

Coleman, Robert. *Evangelism on the Cutting Edge.* Old Tappan:
     Fleming H. Revell, 1986, 82. Quoted in Charles H.
     Nichols, "Communicating to a Biblically Illiterate
     World." *Didaskalia* 4, no. 2 (April 1993): 2-14 [journal
     on-line]; available from OCLC FirstSearch
     ATLAReligion Database,
     http://newfirstsearch.oclc.org; Internet; accessed 2 July
     2006.

Copeland, Mark A. "Biblical Illiteracy." Executable Outlines.
     http://www.ccel.org/contrib/exec_outlines/
     top/bibillit.htm; Internet; accessed 25 May 2006.

Culbertson, Howard. "Why Johnny Can't Read . . . the Bible."
     Southern Nazarene University.
     http://home.snu.edu/~hculbert/flesch.htm; Internet;
     accessed 29 June 2006.

Dalcour, Edward. "The Biblical Illiteracy in the Christian
     Church." Reformation Online.
     http://www.reformationonline.com/illiteracy.htm;
     Internet; accessed 4 July 2006.

Daniel, Lillian. "I Love to Tell the Story to Those Who Know it
     Least: Impact of Biblical Illiteracy Upon Sermon
     Content." *Christianity Today* 43, no. 9 (August 9, 1999):
     49-50 [journal on-line]; available from OCLC
     FirstSearch WilsonSelectPlus Database,
     http://newfirstsearch.oclc.org; Internet; accessed 25
     May 2006.

Filback, Robert and Stephen Krashen. "The Impact of Reading
     the Bible and Studying the Bible on Biblical
     Knowledge." Knowledge Quest: *Journal of the American
     Association of School Librarians* 31, no. 2
     (November/December 2002): 50-51 [journal on-line];
     available from OCLC FirstSearch WilsonSelectPlus
     Database, http://newfirstsearch.oclc.org; Internet;
     accessed 25 May 2006.

Gallup, George. *How Well Do You Know the Bible?* Princeton,
     NJ: Public Opinion News Service. American Institute of
     Public Opinion. PDF, http://brain.gallup.com/
     Braincontent/release/1954_12_19.pdf; Internet;
     accessed 22 July 2006.

Gallup, Jr., George and Frank Newport. *The Bible is Still Widely
     Read and Studied, but Biblical Illiteracy Remains
     Widespread.* Princeton, NJ: The Gallup Poll News
     Service, 55, No. 26a. PDF,
     http://brain.gallup.com/Braincontent/release/1990_1
     1_15.pdf/; Internet; accessed 22 July 2006.

Gelernter, David. "Bible Illiteracy in America." *The Weekly
     Standard,* 010, no. 34 (May 23, 2005) [journal on-line];
     http://www.weeklystandard.com/Content/Public/Ar
     ticles/ 000/000/005/ 606lxblg.asp?pg=1; Internet;
     accessed 25 May 2006.

Greatsite.com. "1455 Gutenberg Bible: The First Book Ever Printed Facsimile Reproduction." Greatsite.com. http://www.greatsite.com/facsimile-reproductions/gutenberg-1455.html; Internet; accessed 24 July 2006.

________. "English Bible History." Greatsite.com. http://www.greatsite.com/timeline-english-biblehistory/index.html; Internet; accessed 24 July 2006.

________. "The Pre-reformation History of the Bible from 1,400 BC to 1,400 AD." Greatsite.com, 2003. http://www.greatsite.com/timeline-english-bible-history/pre-reformation.html; Internet; accessed 24 July 2006.

Hailey, Homer. *A Commentary on Isaiah: With Emphasis on the Messianic Hope.* Grand Rapids, MI: Baker Book House, 1985.

________. *A Commentary on the Minor Prophets.* Grand Rapids, MI: Baker Book House, 1972.

Hogg, William R. "The Scriptures in the Christian World Mission: Three Historical Considerations." *Missiology* 12 (October 1984): 389-404 [journal on-line]; available from OCLC FirstSearch ATLAReligion Database, http://newfirstsearch.oclc.org; Internet; accessed 2 July 2006.

Johnson, Luke Timothy. "Textbook Case: A Bible Curriculum for Public Schools." *The Christian Century* 123, no. 4 (February 21, 2006): 34-37 [journal on-line]; available from OCLC FirstSearch WilsonSelectPlus Database, http://newfirstsearch.oclc.org; Internet; accessed 2 July 2006.

Johnstone, Patrick. *Operation World*, 21st Century Edition. Carlisle, England: Paternoster, 2001, 702. Quoted in Woodrow Kroll, "Crisis in America," Bible Literacy

Center, May 2004.
http://www.bibleliteracycenter.com/articles/4/;
Internet; accessed 25 May 2006.

Knox, Marv, ed. "Baylor Provost's Speech Sparks Debate Over
Baptist Freedom." *The Baptist Standard*, October 18,
2004.
http://www.baptiststandard.com/postnuke/index.ph
p? module=htmlpages&func=display&pid=2401/;
Internet; accessed 24 July 2006.

Kroll, Woodrow. "All Christians Have A Biblical Worldview,
Right?" Bible Literacy Center.
http://www.bibleliteracycenter.com/page_print.php?l
ink=/articles/6/; Internet; accessed 25 May 2006.

_________. "Crisis in America." Bible Literacy Center.
http://www.bibleliteracycenter.com/ articles/4;
Internet; accessed 25 May 2006.

Marlow, Michael. "Ten Steps to Biblical Literacy." Bible
Research. http://www.bible-researcher.com/bible-
study2.html; Internet; accessed 29 June 2006.

Marshall, I. H. *The Book of Acts: An Introduction and
Commentary*. The Tyndale New Testament
Commentaries, ed. Leon Morris, vol. 5. Grand Rapids,
Michigan: William B. Eerdmans Publishing Company,
1980.

Mohler, Albert. "The Scandal of Biblical Illiteracy: It's Our
Problem." Crosswalk.com.
http://crosswalk.com/news/weblogs/mohler/?adate
=06/29/2004; Internet; accessed 4 July 2006.

Nichols, Charles H. "Communicating to a Biblically Illiterate
World." *Didaskalia* 4, no. 2 (April 1993): 2-14 [journal
on-line]; available from OCLC FirstSearch
ATLAReligion Database,
http://newfirstsearch.oclc.org; Internet; accessed 2 July
2006.

Ortiz, Robert W. and Laurie L. McCarty. ""Daddy, Read to Me": Fathers Helping Their Young Children Learn to Read." *Reading Horizons* 38 (November/December 1997): 108-115 [journal on-line]; available from OCLC FirstSearch WilsonSelectPlus Database, http://newfirstsearch.oclc.org; Internet; accessed 2 July 2006.

Percy, Harold. "The Scandal of Biblical Illiteracy." Ministry Matters, January 19, 2004. http://generalsynod.anglican.ca/ministries/departme nts/mm/2004/winter/mm17.html; Internet; accessed 18 July 2006.

Spender, Robert D. "Theology of Hosea," n.p. in *Evangelical Dictionary of Biblical Theology*, [CD-ROM] (PC Study Bible Version 4.3C, Biblesoft, 1996).

The Barna Group, Ltd. "Half of Americans Say Faith Has "Greatly Transformed" Their Life." The Barna Update, June 6, 2006. http://www.barna.org/FlexPage.aspx? Page=BarnaUpdate&BarnaUpdateID=240/; Internet; accessed 23 June 2006.

________. "Only Half Of Protestant Pastors Have a Biblical Worldview." The Barna Update, January 12, 2004. http://www.barna.org/FlexPage.aspx?Page= BarnaUpdate&BarnaUpdateID=156/; Internet; accessed 25 May 2006.

________. "Religious Beliefs Vary Widely By Denomination." The Barna Update, June 25, 2001. http://www.barna.org/FlexPage.aspx?Page=BarnaUp date&Barna UpdateID=92/; Internet; accessed 23 June 2006.

________. "Women are the Backbone of the Christian Congregations in America." The Barna Update, March 6, 2000. http://www.barna.org/FlexPage.aspx?Page= BarnaUpdate&BarnaUpdateID=47/; Internet; accessed 23 June 2006.

________. *The State of the Church: 2006*. Ventura, CA: The Barna Group, Ltd.

The Gallup Organization. *Teenagers' Knowledge of the Bible, The Bible Literacy Report: What Do American Teens Need to Know and What Do They Know?* New York City: Bible Literacy Project, 2005.

Turner, Helen Lee, Amy E. Jones, and Doris A. Blazer. "The Hanna-Barbara Cartoons: Compounding Bible Ignorance." *The Christian Century* 106 (March 1, 1989): 231-234 [journal on-line]; available from OCLC FirstSearch ATLAReligion Database, http://newfirstsearch.oclc.org; Internet; accessed 25 May 2006.

Vlach, Michael. "Crisis in America's Churches: Bible Knowledge at All-time Low." TheologicalStudies.org. http://www.theologicalstudies.citymax.com/page/page/ 1573625.htm; Internet; accessed 15 July 2006.

Web Evangelism Guide. "An Interpersonal Communication Model: The Engle Scale Explained." Gospelcom.net. http://guide.gospelcom.net/resources/tellitoften.php /; Internet; accessed 29 July 2006.

Willis, Jerry. "Correlates of Bible Knowledge." *Journal for the Scientific Study of Religion* 7 (Fall 1968): 280-281 [journal on-line]; available from OCLC FirstSearch ATLAReligion Database, http://newfirstsearch.oclc.org; Internet; accessed 25 May 2006..

Willis, John T. *Isaiah*. The Living Word Commentary on the Old Testament, ed. John T. Willis. Abilene, TX: ACU Press, 1984.

SELECTED BIBLIOGRAPHY

Barna, George. *The State of the Church: 2006.* Ventura, CA: The Barna Group, Ltd., April 2006.

Belfiore, Evelina. "Biblical Illiteracy Affecting the Ministry of Teaching in the Catholic Church." D.Min. diss., Pacific School of Religion, 2001.

Berg, Kay Kupper. "Christian Literacy, the Core Curriculum, and the Urban Church." In *Urban Church Education.* Birmingham, AL: Religious Education Press, 1989.

Bishop, Robert L. "A Survey of Bible Knowledge and Comprehension in 117 Selected Southern Baptist Churches." D.R.E. diss., Southern Baptist Theological Seminary, 1960.

Buchanan, John M, ed. "Schooled in Religion." *The Christian Century* 122, no. 17 (August 23, 2005): 3 [journal on-line]; available from OCLC FirstSearch WilsonSelectPlus Database, http://newfirstsearch.oclc.org; Internet; accessed 2 July 2006.

Burge, Gary M. "The Greatest Story Never Read. Our Biggest Challenge: Recovering Biblical Literacy in the Church." *Christianity Today* 43, no. 9, (August 09, 1999): 45-49 [journal on-line]; available from OCLC FirstSearch ArticleFirst Database, http://newfirstsearch.oclc.org; Internet; accessed 25 May 2006.

Burton-Christie, Douglas. "Listening, Reading, Praying: Orality, Literacy and Early Christian Monastic Spirituality." *Anglican Theological Review* 83, no. 2 (Spring 2001): 197-221 [journal on-line]; available from OCLC FirstSearch ATLAReligion Database, http://newfirstsearch.oclc.org; Internet; accessed 2 July 2006.

Clark, Jerry D. "The Association Between Bible Literacy and
	Religiosity." Ph.D. diss., University of North Texas,
	1991.

Coogan, Michael D. "Literacy and the Formation of Biblical
	Literature." In *Realia Dei*. Atlanta: Scholars Press, 1999.

Copeland, Mark A. "Biblical Illiteracy." Executable Outlines.
	http://executableoutlines.com/top/bibillit.htm;
	Internet; accessed 4 July 2006.

Cragg, Kenneth. ""According to the Scriptures": Literacy and
	Revelation." In *Ways of Reading the Bible*. Sussex, Great
	Britain: Harvester Press, 1981.

Crawford, Jeffrey Scott. "An Analysis of the Biblical Literacy
	of High School Students in Conservative Evangelical
	Schools." Ed.D. diss., Southern Baptist Theological
	Seminary, 2002.

Culbertson, Howard. "Why Johnny Can't Read . . . the Bible."
	Southern Nazarene University. http://home.snu.edu/
	~hculbert/flesch.htm; Internet; accessed 4 July 2006.

Dalcour, Edward. "The Biblical Illiteracy in the Christian
	Church." Reformation Online.
	http://www.reformationonline.com/illiteracy.htm;
	Internet; accessed 4 July 2006.

Daniel, Lillian. "I Love to Tell the Story to Those Who Know it
	Least: Impact of Biblical Illiteracy Upon Sermon
	Content." *Christianity Today* 43, no. 9 (Aug. 9 1999): 49-
	50 [journal on-line]; available from OCLC FirstSearch
	WilsonSelectPlus Database,
	http://newfirstsearch.oclc.org; Internet; accessed 25
	May 2006.

Dawson, Paul C. "Preaching for Biblical Literacy:
	Understanding the Sermon as a Teaching Event."
	D.Min. diss., Brite Divinity School, Texas Christian
	University, 1997.

Degges, Robert Kent. "Confronting Biblical Illiteracy: In
        Dialogue with Text and People." D.Min. diss., Wesley
        Theological Seminary, 1995.

Draper, Jonathan A. "Less Literate are Safer": The Politics of
        Orality and Literacy in Biblical Interpretation."
        Anglican Theological Review 84, no. 2 (Spring 2002): 303-
        318 [journal on-line]; available from OCLC FirstSearch
        ATLAReligion Database,
        http://newfirstsearch.oclc.org; Internet; accessed 2 July
        2006.

Filback, Robert. "The Impact of Reading the Bible and
        Studying the Bible on Biblical Knowledge." Knowledge
        Quest: *Journal of the American Association of School
        Librarians* 31, no. 2 (November/December 2002): 50-51
        [journal on-line]; available from OCLC FirstSearch
        WilsonSelectPlus Database,
        http://newfirstsearch.oclc.org; Internet; accessed 25
        May 2006.

Frame, Randall L. "Is Bible Knowledge Becoming Just
        Another Trivial Pursuit: Inspired by Board Game,
        Entrepreneurs Profit From "Bible Trivia"." *Christianity
        Today* 28, no. 14 (October 5, 1984): 62-63 [journal on-
        line]; available from OCLC FirstSearch ATLAReligion
        Database, http://newfirstsearch.oclc.org; Internet;
        accessed 25 May 2006.

"Freedom to Be Illiterate; We've Gone Nuts in Fear of Faith."
        The Washington Times, 6 June 2005, A23 [database on-
        line]; available from Questia,
        http://www.questia.com/PM.qst?a=o&d=5009525587.
        Internet; accessed 1 June 2006.

Galli, Mark. "Defeating the Conspiracy: Ignorance, Prejudice,
        and Even "Bible" Christianity Joined Forces to
        Sabotage the Faith of African-American Slaves."
        Christian History, no. 62 (1999): 10-17 [journal on-line];
        available from OCLC FirstSearch ATLAReligion

Database, http://newfirstsearch.oclc.org; Internet; accessed 2 July 2006.

________. "The Beginning of Education: The New Bible Literacy Project Curriculum is Impressive as Far as it is Able to Go." *Christianity Today* 49, no. 10 (October 2005): 78-81 [journal on-line]; available from OCLC FirstSearch ATLAReligion Database, http://newfirstsearch.oclc.org; Internet; accessed 25 May 2006.

Gelernter, David. "Bible Illiteracy in America." *The Weekly Standard*, 010, no. 34 (05/23/2005) [journal on-line]; http://www.weeklystandard.com/Content/Public/Articles/000/000/005/ 606lxblg.asp?pg=1 Internet; accessed 25 May 2006.

Griffin, David W. "An Examination and Use of "Disciple: Becoming Disciples through Bible Study" and Evaluation of its Effects on the Biblical Knowledge and Aptitude of Participants." D.Min. diss., Southern Methodist University, 1989.

Guske, Matthew J. "Bible Knowledge Scores between Youth Who Regularly Attend Church and Christian Day School Youth." M.A. thesis, Simpson College, 1992.

Grayston, John. "The Bible and Spirituality: The Decline in Biblical Literacy Among Evangelicals and the Future of the Quiet Time." *Anvil* 19, no. 2 (2002): 99-107 [journal on-line]; available from OCLC FirstSearch ATLAReligion Database, http://newfirstsearch.oclc.org; Internet; accessed 2 July 2006.

Heard, Catherine Pauline. "A Comparison of Bible Knowledge in Home School and Christian School Students." M.A.C.S.E. thesis, Southwestern Baptist Theological Seminary, 2004.

Hogg, William R. "The Scriptures in the Christian World Mission: Three Historical Considerations." *Missiology* 12 (October 1984): 389-404 [journal on-line]; available from OCLC FirstSearch ATLAReligion Database, http://newfirstsearch.oclc.org; Internet; accessed 2 July 2006.

Hunter, Edith. "Woe unto Us Who are Biblically Literate." *Union Seminary Quarterly Review* 8 (January 1953): 12-16 [journal on-line]; available from OCLC FirstSearch ATLAReligion Database, http://newfirstsearch.oclc.org; Internet; accessed 3 July 2006.

"Increasing Biblical Literacy." *Christian Standard* 130, no. 9 (February 26, 1995): 3 [journal on-line]; available from OCLC FirstSearch ArticleFirst Database, http://newfirstsearch.oclc.org; Internet; accessed 25 May 2006.

Johnson, David E. *Opening the New Testament: A Way to Read the Bible in Logical and Historical Order; Towards the Recovery of Biblical Literacy.* Cincinnati, OH: Forward Movement Publications, 1989.

Johnson, Luke Timothy. "Textbook Case: A Bible Curriculum for Public Schools." *The Christian Century* 123, no. 4 (February 21, 2006): 34-37 [journal on-line]; available from OCLC FirstSearch WilsonSelectPlus Database, http://newfirstsearch.oclc.org; Internet; accessed 2 July 2006.

Jones, L. Gregory. "Imagining Scripture." *The Christian Century* 119, no. 13 (June 19-26, 2002): 33 [journal on-line]; available from OCLC FirstSearch WilsonSelectPlus Database, http://newfirstsearch.oclc.org; Internet; accessed 25 May 2006.

Kennedy, D. James and Jerry Newcombe. *What If the Bible Had Never Been Written?* Nashville, TN: Thomas Nelson Publishers, 1998.

Kirsch, Phil. "A Study of the Relationship between Biblical Knowledge and Certain Selected Variables." M.A.C.E. thesis, Western Conservative Baptist Seminary, 1982.

Kirtdoll, Ivy Jo. "Biblical Literacy: Bridging the Gap between Pulpit and Pew through Discipleship Training." D.Min. diss., United Theological Seminary, 1997.

Kroll, Woodrow. "All Christians Have A Biblical Worldview, Right?" Bible Literacy Center. http://www.bibleliteracycenter.com/articles/6; Internet; accessed 25 May 2006.

________. "Crisis in America." Bible Literacy Center. http://www.bibleliteracycenter.com/articles/4; Internet; accessed 25 May 2006.

Matto, Ken. "Christian Ignorance: Is it a Badge of Honor?" Scion of Zion Internet Ministry. http://www.scionofzion.com/christian_ignorance.htm ; Internet; accessed 4 July 2006.

Mattox, William R. "The Bible Is No Laughing Matter." *The American Enterprise* 11, no. 6 (Spring 2000): 8 [journal on-line]; available from OCLC FirstSearch WilsonSelectPlus Database, http://newfirstsearch.oclc.org; Internet; accessed 2 July 2006.

Miller, Stephen R. "A Study of Biblical Literacy Among College Freshmen at a Fundamental Christian University." Doctoral diss., Bob Jones University, 1991.

Moenning, David Clark. "Biblical Literacy Among Baby Busters." D.Min. diss., Asbury Theological Seminary, 2002.

Mohler, Albert. "The Scandal of Biblical Illiteracy: It's Our
Problem." Crosswalk.com.
http://crosswalk.com/news/weblogs/mohler/?adate
=06/29/2004; Internet; accessed 4 July 2006.

Morgan, Richard Lyon. "Scandal of Biblical Literacy."
Christianity Today 9 (May 7, 1965): 5-7 [journal on-line];
available from OCLC FirstSearch ATLAReligion
Database, http://newfirstsearch.oclc.org; Internet;
accessed 2 July 2006.

"Most Americans Take Bible Stories Literally; Accounts More
Than Lessons, Poll Reveals." *The Washington Times*, 17
February 2004, A01 [database on-line]; available from
Questia, http://www.questia.com/PM.qst?
a=o&d=5002076012. Internet; accessed 2 July 2006.

"Move Over National Enquirer – The Bible is Coming: CBN
and Tyndale House Launch a Campaign Against
Biblical Illiteracy." *Christianity Today* 28, no. 8 (May 18,
1984): 77 [journal on-line]; available from OCLC
FirstSearch ATLAReligion Database,
http://newfirstsearch.oclc.org; Internet; accessed 2 July
2006.

Murphey, Cecil B. *The Dictionary of Biblical Literacy: Essential
Information on the Bible, Biblical Culture, and the Church:
Its History, Ideas, and Major Personalities.* Nashville, TN:
Thomas Nelson Publishers, 1989.

Nelson, Daniel. "Bible Knowledge and Moral Judgment:
Knowing Scripture and Using Ethical Reasoning."
Journal of Research on Christian Education 13, no. 1
(Spring 2004): 41-57 [journal on-line]; available from
OCLC FirstSearch WilsonSelectPlus Database,
http://newfirstsearch.oclc.org; Internet; accessed 25
May 2006.

Newport, Frank. "Twenty-Eight Percent Believe Bible Is
Actual Word of God: Ten-point Decline Over Last
Three Decades." Gallup Poll News Service (22 May

2006). http://poll.gallup.com/content/default.aspx?
ci=22885; Internet; accessed 4 July 2006.

Nichols, Charles H. "Communicating to a Biblically Illiterate
World." *Didaskalia* 4, no. 2 (April 1993): 2-14 [journal
on-line]; available from OCLC FirstSearch
ATLAReligion Database,
http://newfirstsearch.oclc.org; Internet; accessed 2 July
2006.

Nicholson, Adam. "The Bible Tells Me So: Biblical Illiteracy is
a Shame." *Opinion Journal* (September 23, 2005) [journal
on-line]; available from
http://www.opinionjournal.com/taste/?id=110007304
; Internet; accessed 4 July 2006.

Ortiz, Robert W. and Laurie L. McCarty. ""Daddy, Read to
Me": Fathers Helping Their Young Children Learn to
Read." *Reading Horizons* 38 (November/December
1997): 108-115 [journal on-line]; available from OCLC
FirstSearch WilsonSelectPlus Database,
http://newfirstsearch.oclc.org; Internet; accessed 2 July
2006.

Osmer, Richard Robert. "Teaching the Catechism in the
Children's Sermon : A New Possibility for Biblical and
Theological Literacy." *Journal for Preachers* 22, no 4
(1999): 37-43 50-51 [journal on-line]; available from
OCLC FirstSearch ArticleFirst Database,
http://newfirstsearch.oclc.org; Internet; accessed 25
May 2006.

Percy, Harold. "The Scandal of Biblical Illiteracy." *Ministry
Matters* (Winter 2004) [journal on-line]; available from
http://generalsynod.anglican.ca/ministries/departme
nts/mm/2004/ winter/mm17.html; Internet; access 4
July 2006.

Peters, Frank C. "The Construction of an Objective
Standardized Bible Knowledge Test." M.S. thesis,
Kansas State Teachers College of Emporia, 1948.

Pike, Patricia L. "Assimilation and Accommodation Applied to Vernacular Scriptures-In-Use." *Journal of Psychology & Theology* 11 (Fall 1983): 189-195 [journal on-line]; available from OCLC FirstSearch ATLAReligion Database, http://newfirstsearch.oclc.org; Internet; accessed 2 July 2006.

Plummer, Minnie Knox. *Basic Bible Foundations: A Literacy Textbook and Study Guide of Old Testament Events.* Authorhouse, 2006.

Reidy, Miriam. "Bible Societies and Literacy: Teaching People to Read." *One World*, no. 171 (December 1991): 16-17 [journal on-line]; available from OCLC FirstSearch ATLAReligion Database, http://newfirstsearch.oclc.org; Internet; accessed 2 July 2006.

Richardson, Brian Craig. "A Critical Evaluation of the Correlation of Bible Knowledge and the Attitudes Southern Baptist Adults Have of Self and Others." Ed.D. diss., Southwestern Baptist Theological Seminary, 1972.

Schatkin, Margaret A. "John Chrysostom: Advocate of Biblical Literacy." In *Historiam Perscrutari*. Roma: Editrice LAS, 2002.

Schippe, Cullen, and Chuck Stetson. *The Bible and Its Influence.* Fairfax, VA: BLP Publishing, 2005.

Searl, Robert M. "Getting the Word in Edgewise: Laying a Foundation for Biblical Literacy for the Youth Group of the University Baptist Church." D.Min. diss., Midwestern Baptist Theological Seminary, 2001.

Sloyan, Gerard S. "Why Ignorance of the Bible Makes Good Liturgical Observance Impossible." *Pastoral Music* 24, no. 1 (October 01, 1999): 25 [journal on-line]; available from OCLC FirstSearch ArticleFirst Database, http://newfirstsearch.oclc.org; Internet; accessed 2 July 2006.

Smart, James. *The Strange Silence of the Bible in the Church: A Study in Hermeneutics*. London: Westminster John Knox Press, 1970.

Smith, James K. A. "The Closing of the Book: Pentecostals, Evangelicals, and the Sacred Writings." *Journal of Pentecostal Theology*, no. 11 (December 1997): 49-71 [journal on-line]; available from OCLC FirstSearch ATLAReligion Database, http://newfirstsearch.oclc.org; Internet; accessed 2 July 2006.

Snoeyink, Arnold. *Bible Literacy Tests: Age Levels 11-15 ; Grade Levels 5-9*. CSI Publications, 1981.

Sohns, Stephen J. "Lack of Comprehensive Bible Study as a Factor in Biblical Illiteracy." M.Div. thesis, Concordia Theological Seminary, Ft. Wayne, 1984.

Stearns, Gladys J. "The Relationship between Biblical Knowledge and Character Conduct of Protestant Bible Class Students of Mesa, Arizona." M.A. thesis, Arizona State College, Flagstaff, 1955.

Streed, John C. "The End of Biblical Literacy." *Perspectives* 12 (January 1997): 6-7 [journal on-line]; available from OCLC FirstSearch ATLAReligion Database, http://newfirstsearch.oclc.org; Internet; accessed 2 July 2006.

Sutherland, Jim. "Developing Biblical Literacy in the Local Congregation." D.Min. diss., Phillips University Graduate Seminary, 1985.

Taylor, Barbara Brown. "Caution: Bible Class in Session. Students' Lack of Knowledge About Bible" *The Christian Century* 119, no. 23 (Nov. 6-19 2002): 39 [journal on-line]; available from OCLC FirstSearch

WilsonSelectPlus Database,
http://newfirstsearch.oclc.org; Internet; accessed 25
May 2006.

Taylor, Mark D. *The Complete Book of Bible Literacy*. Wheaton,
IL: Tyndale House Publishers, 1992.

Telushkin, Joseph. *Biblical Literacy: The Most Important People,
Events, and Ideas of the Hebrew Bible*. New York: William
Morrow, 1997.

The Gallup Organization. *Teenagers' Knowledge of the Bible, The
Bible Literacy Report: What Do American Teens Need to
Know and What Do They Know?* New York City: Bible
Literacy Project, 2005.

Turner, Helen Lee, Amy E. Jones, and Doris A. Blazer. "The
Hanna-Barbara Cartoons: Compounding Bible
Ignorance." *The Christian Century* 106 (March 1, 1989):
231-234 [journal on-line]; available from OCLC
FirstSearch ATLAReligion Database,
http://newfirstsearch.oclc.org; Internet; accessed 25
May 2006.

Vlach, Michael J. "Crisis in America's Churches: Bible
Knowledge at All-Time Low." TheologicalStudies.org.
http://www.theologicalstudies.citymax.com/page/pa
ge/ 1573625.htm; Internet; accessed 4 July 2006.

Wachlin, Marie. *Bible Literacy Report II: What University
Professors Say Incoming Students Need to Know*. Front
Royal, VA: Bible Literacy Project, 2006.

Wallace, Rayford Leon. "A Study of the Effectiveness of
Didactic Preaching in Increasing Knowledge of the
Bible Among Older Church Participants." D.Min. diss.,
Oral Roberts University, 1991.

Wampler, F. Reuel. "A Correlational Study of the Scores of
Mentally Retarded Children and Youth on a Bible

Knowledge Test and a Concepts of God Test." M.S. thesis, Kansas State College of Pittsburg, 1967.

Watkins, Morris. "Literacy, Bible Reading and Church Growth through the Ages." D.Miss. diss., Fuller Theological Seminary, 1978.

Weerstra, Hans M. "Reaching Non-literate Peoples." *International Journal of Frontier Missions* 12 (April-June 1995): 57, 59-68, 71-109 [journal on-line]; available from OCLC FirstSearch ATLAReligion Database, http://newfirstsearch.oclc.org; Internet; accessed 2 July 2006.

Willis, Jerry. "Correlates of Bible Knowledge." *Journal for the Scientific Study of Religion* 7 (Fall 1968): 280-281 [journal on-line]; available from OCLC FirstSearch ATLAReligion Database, http://newfirstsearch.oclc.org; Internet; accessed 25 May 2006.

Wonderly, William L. "Literacy Selections of Biblical Materials." *Bible Translator* 19, no. 2 (April 1968): 58-69 [journal on-line]; available from OCLC FirstSearch ATLAReligion Database, http://newfirstsearch.oclc.org; Internet; accessed 2 July 2006.

Zajac, Mary. "The Comfort of Knowing: An Ethnography of Literacy and Learning in an Adult Catholic Bible Study." Ph.D. diss., University of Illinois at Chicago, 2003.